THE FOUNDING FATHERS AND THE BIRTH OF A NATION STATE

Thomas E. Sawyer, Ph.D., J.D.

THE FOUNDING FATHERS
AND
THE BIRTH OF A NATION STATE

Published in the United States by:
PitBull Literary & Publishing Services
Cary, North Carolina

Library of Congress Control Number: 2020901105

(Paperback) ISBN-13: 978-1-7327371-5-0
(Hard Cover) ISBN-13: 978-1-7327371-6-7

DEDICATION

TO:

THE YOUTH OF AMERICA—MAY YOUR THIRST FOR KNOWLEDGE BE GREAT, AND YOU BE DESERVING OF THE GREAT HERITAGE THAT HAS BEEN BESTOWED UPON YOU.

ACKNOWLEDGEMENTS

The Author, once again, is deeply indebted to his daughter, Kelly, for her outstanding support in publishing this manuscript.

A debt of gratitude also is owed to Jim English, who volunteered to edit the final version of the manuscript prior to its publication.

Love of One's Country Can Only Be Attained Through

Knowledge of Its History

T.E.S.

July 4, 2019

COMMENTARY

The Author's impetus for writing this book is based on, what the author believes to be, a two-fold objective:

1. First and foremost, to attempt to refresh the reader's knowledge and appreciation of the legacy, courage, and sacrifice of our "Forefathers" in founding the establishment of this great nation that we call "The United States of America."

2. To counter the simplistic and "Anti-American" rhetoric of certain political elements in our society who champion views and objectives that are counter to the basic nature of our established political system; namely, that our nation was founded as a "republic" — with governing principles related thereto; i.e., with ultimate power resting with the people and their local governing authorities. Moreover, as espoused by our "Forefathers," governmental power should, and must, originate with the people and flow upward through the governmental establishment—i.e., beginning with the local and state governments upward to the central governing bodies. First and foremost, the governing role of the central governmental bodies should and must be attentive to local governmental interests and the people that they represent. Unfortunately, over the

years, the central governing authorities largely have usurped local governmental authority. Relatedly, the central governing authorities have not only become omnipotent in their governing authority, but have developed into stagnant, bureaucratic relics that achieve no or little resolution of the nation's many problems. Relatedly, their budgetary expenditures, unfortunately, continue to grow and grow; possibly leading this nation to an eventual, budgetary crisis of great proportions.

3. Consequently, this nation is facing a potential crisis of monumental weakness from within; as evidenced not only by the growing budgetary situation, but also by the opposing political environments of the West and East Coasts versus other geographic regions of the United States; such as the Midwest and Southern states. (In other words, citizens of the Midwest and the Southern States are tired of being ruled by the dictates of the West and East Coasts.)

One suggested remedy to lessen our political ills would be the enactment of "term limits" for members of the United States Congress; as well as for the "Executive" and "Judicial" Branches of the National Government. ("Elective Office" should not constitute a "career endeavor" or "life long reality." To the contrary, our "Forefathers," especially James Madison, opposed such a reality.)

The Author

Addendum:

The author recalls that, during the 1970's, there was serious discussion, among "Political Scientists," of the merits of the so-called "Regionalism Concept"; i.e., "The Political Theory of Regional Rather than Central Systems of Administration or Political Affiliation; including having 'regional capitals' as governing units."

Moreover, instead of "all-powerful" Federal Governmental Bodies being "headquartered' in Washington, D.C., these governing units would be relocated to other geographic regions of the United States. For example, the FBI could be headquartered in Atlanta, Georgia; the State Department in New York City; the Department of Defense in Richmond, Virginia; the Interior Department in Colorado; etc. Moreover, the United States Congress also would be affected; possibly in reducing its membership necessary for location in Washington, D.C. In other words, the "Washington Swamp" could be drained substantially. (But, of course, the "National Executive," "National Congress," and "National Judiciary" would still be necessary to govern purely "national affairs"—such as "national security," "national defense," "international trade and relations," and "national judicial issues." For example, the President and his White House Staff, Cabinet Secretaries and small "Staffs," Supreme Court Justices and their Clerks, plus those remaining Congressmen with "Staffs" that serve both Houses of Congress could remain in Washington, D.C.)

Such a dispersal of governmental power should not weaken our governmental efficiency or pose threats to our national security. On the contrary, it might even improve them. Most certainly, it should reduce the national budget considerably. Moreover, with modern transportation and communication systems there should be no threat to our national unity and cohesion. In addition, the present glut of "lobbyists" that pervade the current national scene could be drastically reduced or eliminated altogether. As an added plus, the cost of government should be reduced significantly. (Living costs and wages should be considerably less in other parts of the country. Moreover, individual states and local communities would benefit economically by having these federal offices located in their communities.)

Most important, it is believed that local governing bodies should administer such local needs as the education of youth, health and related insurance programs for their citizens, as well as social programs for the needy, and infrastructure requirements. Most and foremost, the welfare of ordinary citizens will be better served by local governing bodies. For example, local officials will have a better understanding of the needs and desires of their citizens—such as the education of children, health and social programs, infrastructure requirements, etc. Also, their officials will be located close at hand and not located hundreds of miles away in their Washington, D.C., sanctuaries. It is also believed that graft, favoritism, and other unlawful practices will be significantly curtailed as these local governing bodies would be more closely scrutinized by the local citizenry, press, and other societal entities.

Note: Of course, the Author realizes that that there are certain instances in the course of human relations when there are overwhelming realities, such as the recent "Coronavirus Medical Epidemic" where national leadership and control are vital to the welfare of the people and the nation as a whole. However, these incidents, fortunately, are not the norm and, therefore, should not be considered as the paramount criterion for adhering to a highly centralized governmental structure.

Contents

INTRODUCTION

This writing depicts the deliberations of the delegates to the "Federal (Constitutional)Convention of 1787" in Philadelphia; who were charged with the herculean task of establishing a government for the newly established nation-state of "The United States of America." In doing so, to a man, the delegates sought to create a nation unlike any other nation existing up to that time. A nation founded on the principles of individual freedom, liberty, and equal justice for all its citizens before the law. It was a noble experiment that never before had been attempted.

Therefore, although the "book size" of this writing is small, the merits of its contents are huge; the creation of the greatest nation-state in history.

The Author

PREFACE

THE ANNAPOLIS CONVENTION OF SEPTEMBER 11-14, 1786

A ruse was instigated by James Madison to bring about the holding of a Constitutional Convention to replace the inadequate "Articles of Confederation." This deception resulted in the "Annapolis Convention of September 11-14, 1786." (The formal title of the "Annapolis Convention" was "The Meeting of Commissioners To Remedy Defects of the Federal Government.") Although delegates from all the states were invited to Annapolis, only twelve delegates from five states (Delaware, New Jersey, New York, Pennsylvania, and Virginia) attended the Annapolis Convention. (Alexander Hamilton attended the Annapolis convention as a delegate from New York.)

At the Convention, both Madison and Hamilton immediately dismissed the "Articles of Confederation" as being totally inadequate and urged their fellow delegates to seek the convening of a "Constitutional Convention" the following year (1787) in Philadelphia. The other delegates unanimously agreed.

(See, inter alia, https://www.britanica.com/event/Annapolis Convention; https://classroom.synonym.com/Classroom;https://www.us-history.com/pages/H3988.hrmi.)

I. THE PHILOSOPHICAL ANTECEDENCE OF THE AMERICAN APPROACH TO THE "SEPARATION OF POWERS DOCTRINE"

The Doctrine of the "Separation of Powers" and "Institutional Theory" is both a normative and a negative approach to government. The history of Western political thought has emphasized the development and elaboration of a traditional set of values—justice, liberty, equality, and sanctity of property. The great theme of the advocates of "Constitutionalism," in contrast either to theorists of "Utopianism" or "Absolutism," of the right or left, has been the acknowledgement of the role of government in society; linked with the determination to bring government under control and place limits on the exercise of governmental power. Of the theories of government which have attempted to provide a solution to this dilemma, the "Doctrine of the Separation of Powers," in modern times, has been the most significant; both intellectually and in terms of influence on institutional structures.

The "Doctrine of the Separation of Powers" is not a simple and immediately recognizable, unambiguous set of concepts. On the contrary, it represents an area of political thought in which there has been considerable controversy and confusion. In addition, the

"Doctrine of the Separation of Powers," standing alone as a theory of government, has uniformly failed to provide an adequate basis for an effective, stable political system. Consequently, the practicalities of government have necessitated the combining of this doctrine with other political ideas—the theory of "mixed government," the idea of "balanced government," and the concept of "checks and balances"—to form the complex constitutional theories that provide the basis of modern Western political systems. Nevertheless, when all the necessary qualifications have been made, the essential ideas behind the doctrine remain as vital ingredients of Western political thought and practice today. This particularly true in the American political experience; where the principle of the "Separation of Powers" constitutes one of the fundamental foundations of good government.

The "Doctrine of the Separation of Powers" has its beginnings in the ancient world where the concepts of "governmental functions" and the theories of "mixed and balanced government" (representing the various social classes) were evolved. These, I might add, were essential elements in the development of the "Separation of Powers Doctrine." It was in England during the seventeenth and eighteenth centuries, however, in the aftermath of great social upheaval that the doctrine emerged as a response to the need for a new constitutional government; when the system of government based upon a mixture of "King, Lords, and Commons" seemed no longer relevant. The revolutionary potentialities of the "Doctrine of the Separation of Powers," in the hands of opponents of aristocratic privilege and monarchical power, became a powerful weapon for reform. Thus, began the complex interaction between the "Separation of Powers Doctrine" and other constitutional theories; which attained fruition especially in the constitutional development of the emerging American nation state.

The first element of the "Separation of Powers Doctrine" is the assertion of a division of the agencies of government into three categories: the legislature, executive, and judicial. (The earliest versions of the doctrine were, in fact, based on a twofold division of governmental functions; but since the mid-eighteenth century the threefold division is generally accepted as the basic necessity for constitutional government.) This diffusion of authority among different centers of decision-making is the antithesis of "totalitarianism" or "absolutism."

The second element in the doctrine is the assertion that there be three, specific functions of government—a sociological truth that in all governmental situations three necessary functions have to be performed. All governmental acts, it is claimed, can be classified as an exercise of the legislative, executive, and judicial functions. [1]

The third element in the doctrine, and the one which sets the true "Separation of Powers" theorists apart from those who subscribe to the aforementioned general themes, but are not themselves advocates of the "Separation of Powers Doctrine," is the "separation of persons." This is the recommendation that the three branches of government should be composed of quite separate and distinct groups of people; with no overlapping membership. This is the most dramatic characteristic of the "pure" doctrine. This is the most dramatic characteristic of the "pure" doctrine, and is often equated with the "Separation of Powers Theory" as an integral part of that theory.

The final element in the doctrine is the idea that if the governmental authority of specific "agencies," "functions," and "persons" is obeyed then each branch of government would act as a "check" to the arbitrary exercise of power by others, and that each branch, because it is restricted to exercise its own function, would be unable to exercise undue control or influence over other branches.

However, the "Separation of Powers" Theory does not, in itself,

---

[1] M.J.C. Vile, Constitutionalism and the Separation of Powers (Oxford: Clarendon Press, 1967), pp. 1-3.

specify how the power of individual agencies or persons can be restrained. This inadequacy of controls on arbitrary power led to the adaptation of other theories to complement and modify the "Separation of Powers" Theory. The most important of these modifications was the amalgamation of the doctrine of with the theory of "mixed government," or with its later form, the theory of "Checks and Balances" — positive checks to the exercise of power; i.e., each branch was empowered to exercise a degree of direct control over another branch by allowing it to play a limited role in the exercise of the other branch's function. For example, the executive veto power over legislation and the legislative power of executive impeachment. Related to this is the amalgam of the "Doctrine of the Separation of Powers," with the theory of "Mixed Government" to produce a "partial" separation of functions of which Baron de Montesquieu was the original source.

Two further concepts are also closely identified with the "Doctrine of the "Separation of Powers" especially as it evolved in the American application—the idea of "procedure" as a check to the exercise of power; otherwise known as "due process." The other concept is that of "process in government"—-a whole complex of activities which determines the exact manner in which the aforementioned "procedures" will come about; sometimes responsible for achieving the exact opposite of the original purpose.[2]

---

[2] Ibid,., pp. 16-18, 20.

II. AMERICAN EXPONENTS OF THE "SEPARATION OF POWERS DOCTRINE"

From a reading of available historical records and personal writings of the men who were most responsible for forming this government of the United States, it is readily apparent that all were well-educated and well-versed in the political histories and philosophies of Western European culture. It also is apparent that they based their conceptions of the projected American political scheme on the favored European models of the day; i.e., those which advocated the ultimate supremacy of the rule of the people and which provided necessary safeguards against possible usurpations of power by either individual persons or "agencies" of government.

As a consequence of the American revolutionary experience and acquired hatred of British tyrannical practices, the Americans naturally gravitated toward the philosophical teachings of those theorists who advocated "majority rule" and the "Separation of Powers Doctrine"; e.g., John Locke, Baron de Montesquieu, and James Harrington.[3] Locke, it is said, was particularly influential during the days of the active

[3] It is said the American Founders were also influenced by the Swiss constitutional government and especially Swiss theorist Jean Jacques Burlamaqui, author of the Principles of Natural and Political Law; Ray F. Harvey, The Political Philosophy of Jean Jacques Burlamaqui and His Relation to American Constitutional Theory (Chapel Hill: North Carolina University Press, 1937).

revolt against British rule in view of his teachings of "natural rights"; including the "right to revolt." Both Locke and Montesquieu also were influential over the Framers of the American Constitution in their advocacy of the "partial" separation of governmental functions. However, the Montesquieuean idea that the branches of government should represent the dominant social "classes" was rejected. Although Locke neglected the judicial function entirely in his partial "separation of functions" theory, he did project the ideas of a "single person" executive with veto power over legislation, majority rule, and supremacy of the legislature in governmental affairs. Montesquieu enlarged the Lockean approach to good government by advocating a threefold functional division—executive, legislative, and judicial. But, he did not project a "permanent" separate judiciary. The judiciary was to become a strictly American innovation. He also advocated the implementation of a system of "checks and balances."[4]

Most of the Founding Fathers, conservatives and radicals alike, favored the "Separation of Powers Doctrine" as a prime means to protect liberty and the republican form of government. John Adams, considered by many scholars as the most important American theorist during the Revolutionary Period, was one who favored the separation of governmental functions and powers. Although he did not personally participate in the Federal Convention of 1787, due to his official presence in Europe, he did play an active role during the pre-

Convention years in promoting the "Separation of Powers Doctrine" among his contemporaries. Adams, who, for a long time, had wrestled with the problems of government, consulted many authorities; e.g., Aristotle, Locke, Montesquieu, and Harrington, before arriving at any firm philosophical conclusions. As a result of his

---

[4] For details of the Lockean and Montesquieuean theories on the "Separation of Powers" Concept, see John Locke, The Second Treatise of Government, and Baron de Montesquieu, The Spirit of the Laws.

studies, in 1776 Adams wrote his Thoughts on Government Applicable to the Present State of the American Colonies, in which he gave a convincing statement of the "Separation of Powers Principle" at a critical time and copies of which he sent to many American leaders who soon were to be engaged in drafting individual state constitutions and the Federal Constitution. In this pamphlet Adams echoed what he earlier had written in a letter of November 15, 1775, to Richard Henry Lee—"A legislature, an executive, and a judicial power comprehend the whole of what is meant by government. It is by balancing each of these powers against the other two that the efforts in human nature towards tyranny can alone be checked and restrained." John Adams also was for strong executive and judicial branches and for executive veto power over legislation. Although placing considerable emphasis on the separation of powers in his projected form of government, his publication in 1787 of the first volumes of his work, Defence (sic) of the Constitutions of Government of the United States, indicated his actual preference for a mixed form of government (a mixture of monarchy, aristocracy, and democracy).

However, it should be remembered that in his earlier plans for state governments Adams drafted the "State Constitution of Massachusetts" in 1780 in which he developed an outline of a system of "separation of powers" and "checks and balances" which was, in fact, later largely adopted by the Framers of the Federal Constitution.[5]

James Madison, the so-called "Father of the American Constitution," urged and consistently advocated the "Principle of the Separation of Powers" primarily as a defense against despotism. Madison, who was primarily influenced by John Locke and James Harrington, considered the exercise of legislative, executive, and judicial functions by the same person or group of persons as

---

[5] John Adams, Works, 10 vols. (Boston: Little, Brown & Co., 1865), 4:15, 185-87,189,194,205-6; 6:67.

synonymous with tyranny. At the same time, he believed that separation should not be so complete as to preclude any system of "checks and balances" and co-operative efforts between and among the various branches of government.

In the Federal Convention, Madison clearly stated the relationship between the ideas of "separation" and "checks and balances"—"If a constitutional discrimination of the departments on paper were a sufficient security to each against encroachments of the others, all further provisions would indeed be superfluous. But experience had taught us a distrust of that security; and that it is necessary to introduce such a balance of powers and interests as will guarantee the provisions on paper."[6] Madison further noted that ". . . . the accumulation of all powers, legislative, executive, and judicial, in the same hands, whether of one, a few, or many, and whether hereditary, self-appointed, or elective, may justly be pronounced the very definition of tyranny . . ." (The Federalist, No. 47). That same Madison theme is repeated in The Federalist, No. 51—" . . . the great security against a gradual concentration of the several powers in the same department consists in giving to those who administer each department the necessary constitutional means and personal motives to resist encroachment of the others." Madison advocated the "supremacy of the legislature branch" over the other two federal branches (See The Federalist, No. 51) and supported the legislature as "the source of all government policy—" . . . the "whole power of the proposed government is to be in the hands of the representatives of the people. This is the essential and, after all, only efficacious security for the rights and privileges of the people; which is attainable in civil society." He, nevertheless, was fearful of the sovereignty of the majority and sought to implement institutional "checks and balances" in the Federal Government to

---

[6] Charles C. Tansill, Documents Illustrative of the Formation of the American States (Washington, D.C.: Government Printing Office, 1927), p. 333.

prevent domination by any agency or persons representative of the "popular will" (The Federalist, Nos. 28 and 48).

Primarily as a safeguard against "governmental tyranny" and, to a lesser extent, "tyranny by the majority," Madison advocated a bicameral national legislature; the "Senate" acting as an "auxiliary precaution" against the possible usurpation of power by the "Lower House," either acting on its own or on the behalf of a "misguided majority." (See The Federalist, No. 63).[7]

In that regard, Madison particularly was concerned over the potential power of the "Lower House" since it "alone has access to the pockets of the people, and . . . a prevailing influence over the pecuniary rewards of those who fill the other departments; a dependence is thus created in the latter, which gives greater facility to encroachments of the former.[8]

Madison's position on "executive privilege" was largely motivated by his fear of tyranny; especially "governmental tyranny." Consequently, in urging constitutional limitations on the powers of the "Chief Executive," he was more consistent than in other areas of his views on government. (Madison altered some of his views in the "Post-Convention Period" in the face of regional, political realities.) But he also was equally apprehensive over possible legislative encroachment on that he considered strictly executive functions; e.g., the executive rights of tenure of office, appointments, and removal of federal officers. With specific reference to the question of tenure, Madison believed that a President should be able to succeed himself in office, and that no constitutional barriers should be erected in that regard. However, on virtually every aspect of foreign relations Madison was distrustful of executive authority. Madison also was in favor of executive veto power over legislation; whereby a three-fourths' vote in both "Houses" was required to override it.

---

[7] Ibid., pp. 424-25.

[8] ibid., p. 334. Also, The Federalist , No. 48.

On the question of "judicial prerogative" (See The Federalist, No. 78), Madison , like most of the membership of the Convention, conceived of all governmental authority as limited by a superior law derived partly from reason and the order of nature, and partly from the ultimate sovereigns who formed the political compact. He regarded the Federal Constitution as an expression of that law; and he considered the courts to be better qualified than any other agencies of government to expend the constitution, and, therefore, should be charged with the responsibility of maintaining it and protecting the individuals who are under that general body of abstract rights. He therefore was for a strong judiciary; however, he placed a restriction on the Court as a final authority in controversies between departments of government. He believed that each department should determine its own scope of functions according to its own interpretation of the Constitution; which it was equally bound to support with the other departments of government. "The Supreme Court . . . should have no authority to question the judgment of congress concerning what would be a valid exercise of legislative power . . . .If the Court were to have the final word on every question of a constitutional nature, there might be some danger that the republican form of government would be perverted into an oligarchy . . ."[9]

(See Georgetown University Professor Dr. George W. Carey's unpublished paper, "A Separation of Powers & The Madisonian model: A Reply to Critics," for a detailed analysis of the Madisonian model.)

In his book, Alexander Hamilton and the Constitution, Clinton Rossiter makes the basic thesis that, without Hamilton, the

---

[9] Max Farrand, ed., The Records of the Federal Convention of 1787, 3 vols. (New Haven: Yale University Press, 1937), 1:74, 108; 2:34-35, 298; Edward McNall Burns, James Madison, Philosopher of the Constitution (New Brunswick, N.J. : Rutgers University Press, 1938), pp. 169-70.

Constitution, despite the efforts of men like Madison, Washington, Wilson, and Franklin, might never have gotten off the ground; or, even if successfully launched, would certainly have moved off in a different direction. "In other words," said Rossiter, "We live today under a Hamiltonian Constitution."

Hamilton was for a strong "Chief Executive"; to serve "during good behaviour" (sic), and like Madison, Hamilton acknowledged dimensions to executive power beyond the delineation of stated executive powers in Article II of the Constitution. He pushed for the idea of an "energetic" President and, in fact, devoted several of his Federalist essays to that concept:

"Energy in the executive is a leading character in the definition of good government. It is essential to the protection of the community against foreign attacks . . . A feeble executive implies a feeble execution of the government. A feeble execution is but another phrase for a bad execution: And a government ill-executed, whatever it may be in theory, must be in practice a bad government." (The Federalist, No. 70)

Hamilton also claimed a number of implicit powers involved in executive authority. For example, in The Federalist, No. 72, he mentioned the conduct of foreign negotiations and preparing plans of finance as two examples of "implied executive power." However, Hamilton also urged shared executive-legislative control over two important areas of governmental power—the making of treaties with foreign governments, and the removal of officials from the Executive Department.

"The power of making treaties is, plainly, neither the one [legislature] nor the other [executive]: It relates neither to the execution of the subsisting laws nor to the enaction of new ones; and still less to an exertion of the common strength. Its objects are CONTRACTS with foreign nations; which have the force of laws, but derive from it from the obligations of good faith. They are not rules prescribed by sovereign to the subject, but agreements between sovereign and sovereign. The power in question seems therefore to form a distinct department, and to belong, properly, neither to the legislature nor to the executive. (The Federalist, No. 75)

It has been mentioned as one of the advantages to be expected from the co-operation of the Senate, in the business of appointments, that it would contribute to the stability of the administration. The consent of that body would be necessary to displace as well as to appoint. A change of the Chief Magistrate, therefore, would not occasion so violent or so general a revolution in the officers of the government as might be expected; if he were the sole disposer of offices. When a man, in any station, had given satisfactory evidence of his fitness for it, a new President would be restrained from attempting to a change in favor of a person more agreeable to him, by the apprehension that a discountenance of the Senate might frustrate his attempt, and bring some degree of discredit upon himself. Those, who best estimate the value of a steady administration, will be most disposed to prize a provision which connects the official existence of public men with the approbation or disapprobation of that body, which, from the greater permanency of its own composition, will, in all probability, be less subject to inconstancy than any other member of the government. (The Federalist, No. 77)

Hamilton also was in favor of a strong judiciary; empowered to interpret the Constitution; the "fundamental law of the land."

"The interpretation of the law is the proper and peculiar province of the courts. A constitution is, in fact, and must be regarded by the judges as, a fundamental law. It therefore belongs to them to ascertain its meaning as well as the meaning of any particular act proceeding from the legislative body. If there should happen to be an irreconcilable variance between the two, that which has the superior obligation and validity ought, of course, to be preferred; or, in other words, the Constitution ought to be preferred to the statute, the intention of the people to the intention of their agents." (The Federalist , No. 78)

Thomas Jefferson's support of the "Separation of Powers Principle" had much to do with the future use of that principle in the American context because Jefferson best stated the position of the American "radical" element and later became the central figure in the practical politics of the democratic school. Subsequent to his tenure as the second governor of the State of Virginia, Jefferson, in his Notes on the State of Virginia, made the most widely read, inspiring statement of the "Principle of the Separation of Powers" (and also of "Checks and Balances") ever made in America.[10]

Prior to his becoming governor, Jefferson advocated the centralization of authority in the hands of the legislature in the tradition of Rousseau, Mirabeau, and Thomas Paine. Also, in drafting a constitution for the State of Virginia during his stay in Philadelphia in 1776, Jefferson placed emphasis on the powers the executive could not have. He denied the executive the power of veto as well as a long list of prerogatives; which he wanted to grant to the legislature alone. However, his draft did provide that the legislative, executive, and judicial powers should be separate; the executive was granted extensive powers of appointment; there were elaborate provision for setting up courts; and amendments could be secured only by unanimous consent of both houses of the legislature. However, as a result of executive difficulties experienced during his term of office as governor, Jefferson, in the aforementioned Notes on the State of Virginia, used the

---

[10] He noted, for example, that the purpose of the patriots in Virginia had been to create a new system of government in which the powers should be divided and balanced "as that no one could transcend their legal limits; without being checked and restrained by the others." (See Thomas Jefferson, Notes on the State of Virginia, p. 195.)

"Separation of Powers Doctrine" to justify the stronger executive, which he had found necessary as a result of his gubernatorial experience.

In the same writing, Jefferson assailed the Virginia Legislature as characterizing "precisely the definition of despotic government." It was in that same treatise that Jefferson wrote his often quoted remark that it did not make any difference that such despotic powers were vested in a numerous body "chosen by ourselves." . . . . One hundred and seventy-three despots were as oppressive as one . . ."[11]

General George Washington, the "Commander-in-Chief," who was to become the first "President of the United States," did more than any other individual to place a strong executive department into the "Constitution of the United States." The strong, steady purpose of Washington was to secure liberty by means of the supremacy of the law. This made Washington one of the main constitutional architects for the "Separation of Powers Principle"; although he went no further than to establish executive power, respect for the legislative branch, and add his prestige to the respect for the law.

Washington spoke little at the "Constitutional Convention" in Philadelphia. Nevertheless, he had the satisfaction of knowing that his two main convictions were included in the constitutional formula: the stronger national government provided security to the new Republic; and the separation of powers among the legislature, executive, and judicial branches prevented despotic government. Moreover, his years as the first President would establish the precedents required for a

---

[11] During his later years, Jefferson was to become a progressively stronger advocate of the "pure doctrine" of the "Separation of Powers Concept." In fact, he, ultimately, favored the popular election and frequent electoral sanction of all three departments of government. Thomas Jefferson, The Papers of Thomas Jefferson , ed. Julian P. Boyd, 5 vols. (Princeton University Press, 1950-), 1:129, 340-45; idem, The Writings of Thomas Jefferson, ed. Paul L. Ford, 10 vols. (New York: G.P. Putnam's Sons, 1904), 2:160ff, 3:223-24, 235, 333, 454.

strong executive and lawful government.[12]

Patrick Henry never made any specific statements with regard to the "Separation of Powers Doctrine"; but he did express general agreement with John Adams' views on that topic whose Thoughts on Government Applicable to the Present State of the American Colonies was received by Henry. Moreover, Henry was among those appointed to prepare a "Declaration of Rights" and a "Plan of State Government" in the Virginia State Constitutional Convention in 1776. He took that occasion to make an unsuccessful attempt to vest the State Executive with veto power over legislation. Also, during his tenure as the first governor of the State of Virginia, Henry exerted strong executive privileges; interpreting his powers generously and meeting the problems that arose. In the debates in Virginia over the ratification of the Federal Constitution, Henry opposed the Constitution because it created a consolidated government. Although he did not oppose the "Separation of Powers" in the Constitution, he did oppose the control of military by the President as dangerous to liberty because "an ambitious person of address could make himself absolute."[13]

---

[12] George Washington, The Writings of George Washington, ed. John C. Fitzpatrick, 39 vols. (Washington, D.C.: Library of Congress, 1931-44), 3:228, 231,246,291: 29:409-10.

[13] John Adams, Works, 4:201; Patrick Henry, Life, Correspondence and Speeches , ed. William Wirt, 3 vols. (New York: B. Franklin, 1969), 3:452.

III. INFLUENCES ON THE FOUNDING FATHERS IN PHILADELPHIA

The Constitutional Convention in Philadelphia was precipitated, in large measure, by the dismal failure of the "Articles of Confederation" to provide the necessary governmental structure to provide for the efficient management of the emerging national government. In particular, the lack, by the "Articles of Confederation," of a national executive, its inadequate grant of powers to the Congress, and the weakness of its financial support for the national government made revision a necessity. Hence, the establishment of a new and efficient national government was vital for the future of the fledging republic.

That reality also was influenced, to a large degree, by the events that had transpired prior to the delegates' meeting in Philadelphia; i.e., the realities of the revolution and its hardships, the inadequacies of the individual state constitutions, the heavy burden that had just been thrust upon them in launching a new national government, and the threatening dangers of the world around them.

When attempts by the colonies to secure their rights within the British Empire failed, they searched for a fundamental law that would limit Parliament. This reality resulted in written constitutions for every state except Connecticut and Rhode Island; which merely left their colonial charters intact. Six states –New Hampshire, Massachusetts,

Virginia, Maryland, North Carolina, and Georgia—inserted a general clause in their individual state constitutions distributing the powers of government.[14]

The "Distribution Clause" of Maryland was the simplest and most unqualified; that of Massachusetts, the most explicit. The Maryland "Clause" stated that the "legislative, executive, and judicial powers of government ought to be forever separate and distinct from each other." The Massachusetts Clause stated that: "In the government of this Commonwealth, the Legislative Department shall never exercise the Executive and Judicial powers, or either of them; the Executive shall never exercise the Legislative and Judicial powers, or either of them; the Judicial shall never exercise the Legislative and Executive powers, or either of them; to the end it may be a government of law and not of men."

The state constitutions show how difficult it was to give the popular "Separation of Powers" practical application. There was no other theory that stated; yet only a very broad definition of that theory covers the actual structure of the early state constitutions. The several states' recognition of the "Separation of powers Doctrine" was largely verbal—its material terms remained undefined. This was especially true with regard to the relationship between "legislative power" and "judicial power." The state legislatures throughout this period freely vacated judicial proceedings, suspended judicial actions, annulled or modified judgments, cancelled executions, reopened controversies, authorized appeals, granted exemptions from the standing law, etc. Some states withheld equity powers from their courts altogether; while others granted them but sparingly. In no state constitution were the

---

[14] In the "Colonial Charters" there was little, if any, trace of the "Separation of Powers Principle." See Francis L. Thorpe, The Federal and State Constitutions, Colonial Charters, and Other Organic Laws, 7 vols. (Washington, D.C.: Government Printing Office, 1907).

executive and judicial branches given explicitly necessary power; i.e., the power of appointment for the executive and the power of final judicial review for the judicial. However, all states provided for three separate departments of government and gave each some distinct powers of authority.

As the Americans rewrote their state constitutions and attempted to abide by them in everyday life, they became more and more aware of the inadequacies of these instruments of government and the need for certain revisions in them. In that regard, the New York State Constitution of April 20, 1777, largely drafted by John Jay, was especially important; not only in its considerable influence on the men who drafted the Federal Constitution in 1787, but also because it was the first state constitution to depart from the practice of having the legislature elect the executive. Also, the New York Constitution created three independent branches with sufficiently separated powers according to later interpretation of that theory. Moreover, it marked the beginning of the reaction against the extreme rejection of the "Checks and Balances" role. In addition, the New York experience was largely influenced by an executive, Governor George Clinton, whose strong leadership played a role in influencing later conceptions of executive powers. A strong executive role was also being strengthened by the other states not only by strong executives, but also by legislative action to encourage that trend.

The Founding fathers in Philadelphia were, no doubt, influenced by the various court actions; which had strengthened the other judicial departments in the individual states prior to 1787. In several states the judiciary had successfully claimed the power to make decisions on the basis of the individual state constitutions as the fundamental law; i.e., to decide whether given legislation was constitutional or not.[15]

---

[15] Allan Nevins, The American States During and After the Revolution 1775-1789 (New York: Macmillan Co., 1924) pp.161-64. All state constitutions are found in

Consequently, by the time of the Federal Constitution, the two most central positions of modern American constitutional thought were already accepted; "Separation of Powers" and "Checks and Balances."

Thorpe, Federal and State Constitutions ; Briton Cox, An Essay on Judicial Power and Un-Constitutional Legislation: Being a Commentary on Parts of the Constitution of the United States, (Philadelphia: Kay and Brother 1893), p. 220; Edward S. Corwin, American Constitutional History, ed. Alpheus T. Mason and Gerald Garvey (Gloucester, Mass.: Peter Smith, 1970) pp.4, 6.

IV. THE CONSTITUTIONAL CONVENTION OF 1787 AND THE BIRTH OF A NEW NATION STATE: "THE UNITED STATES OF AMERICA"

Note:

In discussing the Constitutional Convention of 1787, the Author would remiss if he did not comment on certain realities of the Colonial era—in particular, the primitive nature of colonial travel and transportation. First of all, the modes of travel and transportation were limited to horseback, coach or carriage, riverboats, and, ultimately walking. Travel, therefore, usually was a time consuming affair; taking hours, days, weeks, months, and even longer. Moreover, travel, over a distance, required nighttime lodgings in an inn, tavern, or other shelter. Long distance travel, of course, was particularly exhausting. So, consider the plight of the delegates to the Philadelphia Convention; particularly those delegates from the northern most and southern most states. In addition, upon arrival in Philadelphia, the delegates were obliged to seek lodgings, for the duration of the Convention, at inns, taverns, rooming houses, and, in individual cases, in private homes. Besides the travel and lodging burdens, the delegates also had to contend with the exceptional heat and humidity of the Philadelphia summer that was increased tenfold by the necessity of closing and locking all the doors and windows of the Convention Hall in order to keep their, oftentimes, boisterous deliberations from being overheard by the outside public. Despite these burdens, however, these exceptional men pressed forward; accomplishing the difficult task that destiny had thrust upon them.

Soon after the convening of the delegates, the Federal Convention became embroiled in the task of outlining the proper spheres and powers of the individual branches of the envisaged Republican government. About this, there remained much controversy, although most , if not all, of the delegates were committed to some form of "separation of powers" and functions. The overriding objective of the Framers, however, was to create a government "to operate directly upon the "People"; and not upon the states.[16]

The "Virginia Plan," submitted on May 30, 1787, immediately after the task of organization of the Convention proceedings had been completed, called for three branches of government; a two-house legislature, the "First Branch" elected by the people of the several states, the "Second Branch" chosen by the House; an executive, selected by the national legislature and ineligible for a second term; and a federal judiciary comprised of a supreme court and inferior courts; chosen by the national legislature to hold office "during good behavior." In the ensuing debate, Roger Sherman of Connecticut wanted the first branch of the legislature to be elected by the various state legislatures. Elbridge Gerry of Massachusetts seconded the Sherman position. However, George Mason of Virginia argued that "the appointment of the legislature coming from the people would make the representation actual, but if it came from the State Legislatures it will be only virtual."

---

[16] Gaillard Hunt and James Brown Scott, The Debates in the Federal Convention of 1787 Which Framed the Constitution of the United States of America (New York: Oxford University Press, 1920), p. 599.

James Wilson of Pennsylvania and James Madison favored the election of one branch of the national legislature (Madison specified the first branch.) by the people.[17]

The aforementioned "Randolph Plan" (named after the Governor of Virginia who introduced the Plan at the convention), which served as the skeletal plan for the proposed Constitution, called for an executive who would be given a "general authority to execute the National laws" and also suggested that such an authority "ought to enjoy the Executive rights vested in Congress by the Confederation."[18]

At Philadelphia the matter of executive authority was one of the most contested issues of the whole Convention. Considerable debate was devoted, first of all, to the composition of the executive, whether it should be single or plural in nature, and also to the manner in which the executive was to be chosen. Charles C. Pinckney, James Wilson, and John Rutledge favored a simple and "vigorous" executive. Wilson, in particular, was concerned over the capacity of the executive to defend itself if animosities were to "run high between the Executive and Legislative branches." Roger Sherman thought that the executive should be appointed by the national legislature. Elbridge Gerry favored his selection by the state executives, and James Wilson opted for his selection by the people.

In the ensuing debate, Elbridge Gerry favored annexing a council to the Executive to "give weight & inspire confidence," and serve as the "medium through which the feelings of the people" would be

---

[17] Tansill, Illustrative Documents, pp. 87-88, 953-63.

[18] Ibid. , p. 87. Just what the Randolph Plan meant by "executive rights" is not clear since the Articles of Confederation allowed for no distinct executive other than a committee to be appointed by Congress to sit during Congressional recess and "manage the general affairs of the United States." The powers given Congress under the Articles of Confederation were not catalogued as either executive or legislative. See Merrill Jensen, The Articles of Confederation: An Interpretation of the Social-Constitutional History of the American Revolution, 1774-1781 (Madison: University of Wisconsin Press, 1948).

communicated to the President. James Madison was also for the council idea, but would allow the President the freedom to accept the advice or not. Wilson was against the proposal. Butler favored a single executive since he felt there would be disunity if the Executive were composed of several equals. (The "council proposal" subsequently was rejected by the Convention delegates.)[19]

Three weeks after the Randolph Plan was proposed, the "Committee of the Whole," on June 14, 1787, passed a resolution to establish a national government consisting of a supreme legislature, and executive, and a judiciary. The national executive was to be given three specified powers: the power to execute the national laws, the power of appointment, and the power of legislative veto, unless overridden by two-thirds of each branch of the national legislature. Also, the executive was to be single in nature and chosen for a seven-year term by the national legislature.

George Mason was against investing the power of appointment in the hands of the President alone. He proposed the creation of a "Presidential Privy Council" of six members chosen for a term of six years by the Senate. Two members would come out of the "Eastern, two out of the Middle, and two out of the Southern quarters of the Union and to go out (of office) in rotation; two every second year. Mason also proposed that the concurrence of the Senate would only be required for the appointment of ambassadors and in making treaties. James Wilson backed the Mason "Privy Council" proposal; provided the advice given was not "obligatory" on the President. Rufus king was against the proposal since "it would create a new corps which must increase expence (sic) as well as influence of the Government." Dickenson was for the proposal as well was Dr. Franklin, who saw it as a further check on presidential power. The proposal subsequently was

---

[19] Farand, Debates, 1:66, 70, 74, 88-89; Tansill, Illustrative Documents, pp. 131-32.

rejected by the Convention. [20]

In the extended debate on the executive branch, there appeared to be general agreement among the delegates with regard to the notion of a "weak" executive; generated by the genuine fear of executive tyranny (sensitized by the Colonies' experience with British rule.) In that regard, Dr. Franklin noted his opposition to absolute veto power for the executive because of the Pennsylvania experience whereby the Governor had extorted money for approving legislation. Roger Sherman also voiced his objection to the proposed executive absolute veto power; as did James Madison, George Mason, Gunning Beford of Delaware, and Pierce butler of South Carolina. (Mason and Randolph were also against the proposal of a single executive because of its monarchical inferences.) Most delegates favored a "qualified" executive veto.

With regard to the Presidential veto power, mention should be made of the so-called "Randolph Resolution" (First Clause, Eighth Resolution), which:

> "Resolved, That the (national) executive and a convenient number of the national judiciary ought to compose a council of revision, with authority to examine every act of the national legislature, before it shall operate, and every act of a particular legislature before a negative thereon shall be final; and that the dissent of the said council shall amount to a rejection, unless the act of the national legislature be again passed, or that of a particular legislature be again negative by ( ) of the members of each branch."

A similar concept was provided in the "Pinckney Plan," which was submitted to the Convention on May 29, 1787. Resolution Six of that

---

[20] Tansill, Illustrative Documents, pp. 131-32, 148-51; Hunt and Scott, Debates in the Federal Convention, pp. 527-29, 531-32.

Plan called for a "Council of Revision" composed of the President, Secretary for Foreign Affairs, Secretary of War, Heads of the Departments of Treasury and Admiralty or "any two of them together with the President."

According to "Notes on the Convention" by George Mason, the Council of Revision concept "was invested, in a great measure, with a power of negative upon the laws; and that this council . . . be formed out of Judiciary (Departments) joined with Executive (Departments)."

Elbridge Gerry was against the aforementioned "Council of Revision" proposal since he doubted whether the Judiciary should be part of it since the Judiciary would have a significant check against encroachments on their own department by their exposition of the laws; which involved a power of deciding on their constitutionality.

Gerry consequently countered with the motion "that the right of revision should be in the Executive only." James Wilson, however, was for joint Executive/Judiciary membership on the Council; otherwise "they cannot preserve their importance against the legislature." Rufus King was against the proposal; Dr. Franklin was for it since he was against absolute Presidential veto power and opined that the Judiciary "should be joined with the Executive to revise the laws." James Madison also favored the proposal since it ". . .would be strictly proper, and would by no means interfere with that indepence (sic) so much to be approved and distinguished in the several departments." Dickinson, on the other hand, could not agree in blending the Judicial with the Executive because "the one is the expounder, and the other the Executor of the Laws." Bedford was against any check on the legislature; even by the "Council of Revision." The "Council of Revision" proposal was rejected by the Convention delegates.[21]

---

[21] Tansill, Illustrative Documents, pp. 752-53, 958; Hunt and Scott, Debates in the Federal Convention, pp. 596-97; Farand, Debates, 1:94, 97-100, 105, 107, 109, 110-11, 131; James Madison, Notes of Debates in the Federal Convention of 1787,

The second major plan was the so-called "Patterson Plan"; which was submitted before the Convention on June 15, 1787. (The "Plan" was named after delegate William Patterson of New Jersey, who introduced the plan.) The "Patterson Plan" called for the enlargement of Congressional powers under the Articles of Confederation; the executive was to be selected by the Congress, and a federal judiciary, consisting of a "Supreme Tribunal," was to be established. The debate over Patterson's Plan never seemed designed seriously to consider implementing it. Rather, it served as a means to limit the Randolph Plan—focusing on the enlargement of the Articles of Confederation, and to bring about what the smaller states considered the tasks of the delegates to Philadelphia to be. [22]

On June 18, 1787, Alexander Hamilton, "hitherto silent on the business before the Convention, partly from respect to others whose superior abilities, age & experience rendered him unwilling to bring forward ideas dissimilar to theirs, and partly from his delicate situation with respect to his own State, to whose sentiments, as expressed by his Colleagues, he could by no means accede, "presented his own plan to the convention. The "Hamilton Plan" constituted a radically different approach to the constitutional situation; on which would have a profound effect on future American generations. Briefly, the "Hamilton Plan" proposed a two-House national legislature with the power to pass "all acts whatsoever," an independent executive elected by electors chosen by the people and possessing an "absolute" veto power over all legislation, and a supreme judiciary. The executive would also have the "sole power of appointment" of the heads of Finance, War, and Foreign Affairs; to make all treaties with the advice

---

with an introduction by Adrienne Koch (Athens: Ohio State University Press, 1966), pp. 59-70.

[22] Tansill, Illustrative Documents, pp.203-07, 329, 967-78; James Madison, Notes, 337-39.

and approbation of the Senate; to direct war when authorized or begun; to nominate all other officers subject to approbation or rejection by the Senate; and to pardon all offense, except treason which needs approval by the Senate. The Senate, executive, and judiciary would serve "during good behavior."[23]

The question of the selection and term of office of the executive constituted one of the most controversial issues before the Convention. The whole matter was tied into the manner in which the executive was to be chosen. As long as the sentiment of the majority of the delegates favored the election of the executive by the national legislature, that majority also favored a single term of seven years. To do otherwise, to allow re-eligibility along with this mode of selection, would, according to such delegates as George Mason and Elbridge Gerry, invite "intrigue and collusion" between the executive and legislative branches. Said Gerry on July 19, 1787, "If the Executive is to be elected by the Legislature, he certainly ought not to be re-eligible. This would make him absolutely dependent." Once the issue was resolved late in the Convention in favor of the election of the executive by electors chosen by the people from the several states, and of a four-year term of office, opposition to executive 're-eligibility' collapsed. [24]

On August 6, 1787, the "Committee of Detail," which included neither Hamilton nor Madison, reported to the Convention a constitutional draft containing the provision that the "executive power" shall be vested in a single person. Following that contention came a list

---

[23] Tansill, Illustrative Documents, pp. 215-25, 979-88.

[24] It was decided by September 12, 1787, on a four-year executive term of office chosen by electors and that each state shall "in such a manner as the legislature thereof (of the individual states) may direct, a number of electors, equal to the whole number of senators and representatives to which the state may be entitled in Congress; but no senator or representative shall be appointed an elector, nor any person holding an office of trust or profit under the United States." Ibid., p. 708; Madison, Notes , pp. 49, 327, 590-93.

of specified powers: for example, power to give information about the "State of the Union" and to make recommendations to the Congress, to receive ambassadors, to grant reprieves and pardons, and the power to be "Commander-In-Chief" of the army, navy, and militia of the several states.

Madison objected to this draft because the executive was not included in the power to make treaties, which the "Committee of Detail" had vested entirely with the Senate. By September 8, 1787, the proposed draft was amended to include the executive in the treaty-making power. No other discussion took place over executive power. The final draft was presented to the Convention on September 12; a draft in which both Hamilton and Madison had taken part. It was accepted without discussion as far as the provisions dealing with the executive branch was concerned.

The respective roles of the executive and the Senate in the treaty-making procedure, however, remained vague and confused. According to delegate Charles C. Pinckney, the discussions at the Convention over the treaty-making procedure, however, were vague and confused. According to delegate Charles C. Pinckney, the discussions at the Convention over the treaty-making powers touched off heated debates. It was "one of those difficult points which, for long-time, occasioned much debate in the Convention." It was argued that that the necessity of secrecy and dispatch in treaty negotiations warranted against vesting such a power in the legislature. However, it also was argued that to vest this power solely with the executive would make the executive susceptible to foreign bribery. Finally, after much debate, "It was agreed to give the President a power of making treaties, as he was the ostensible "Head of the Union," and to vest the Senate (where each state had an equal voice) with the power of agreeing or disagreeing to the terms proposed."

George Mason of Virginia was concerned that the Senate could take the initiative in making treaties—"Five states might a treaty," he charged before the Virginia Ratification Convention; "ten senators, the representatives of five states, being two-thirds of a quorum. These ten might come from the smallest states. By the 'Articles of Confederation,' nine states were necessary to concur in a treaty. This secured justice and moderation." Now, he argued, "A bare majority would make treaties to bind the Union."

Alexander Hamilton argued for the power of the executive to continue or suspend treaties. Madison argued against this since it would allow the executive to encroach upon the exclusive Congressional authority to declare war.

When one reads the records of the debates at Philadelphia, the impression seems quite strong that the Madisonian view probably represented more the prevailing attitude of the delegates at the Convention. There appeared to be a consensus at the Convention that executive powers should not be too great, and that vigilance should be maintained over increased executive powers particularly in times of crisis. One strong argument against the creation and maintenance of a standing national army was that such a military establishment would strengthen executive power since the Chief Executive was the "Commander-in-Chief." That fear was expressed by Edmund Randolph who noted that "The Executive will have great opportunity of abusing his power particularly in time of war when the military force . . .will be in his hands."[25]

Three delegates at Philadelphia did not sign the Constitution, two of these being George Mason and Elbridge Gerry, in part because the

---

[25] Madison, Notes, pp. 334, 392-93, 520, 575; Jonathan Elliot, The Debates in the Several State Conventions on the Adoption of the Federal Constitution , 5 vols. 3[d] ed. (Philadelphia: J.B. Lippincott Co., 1901) , 3:264-65, 499; Alexander Hamilton, The Works of Alexander Hamilton, ed. Henry Cabot Lodge, 12 vols. (New York: G.P. Putnam's Sons, 1904), 4:441-42.

Constitution excluded the House of Representatives in the treaty-making role. (Mason also was concerned about the lack of the proper separation of powers and what was, to him, a dangerous blending of executive and legislative powers.) Gouverneur Morris proposed that no treaty should become binding until after it had been ratified by a subsequent law; thus, involving the entire Congress in its subsequent effectuation. The Morris proposal was defeated by an eight-to-one vote.

In opposing the measure, Nathaniel Gorham of Massachusetts noted that such a proposal would produce procedural confusion on the part of the American representatives abroad. Such representatives would go abroad instructed by one authority (presumably, the President and the Senate) and then come back and depend on another authority (full Congress) to "ratify their proceedings."

James Madison proposed that treaties should be "classified" and that the President and the Senate should be exclusively concerned with one type (of treaty); whereas the whole Congress would have to concur in another type. (Madison was somewhat unclear on this particular topic.)

Finally, late in the Convention, on September 7, James Wilson proposed an amendment that would explicitly include the House of Representatives in the treaty-making process. Said Wilson, "As treaties . . . are to have the operation of laws, they ought to have the sanction of laws also." Roger Sherman objected. He believed that such a power could be "safely trusted to the Senate." The necessity for secrecy in treaty-making, he claimed, forbade a reference of treaties to the whole legislature. The Wilson motion was soundly defeated by a ten-to-one vote.[26] (The records of the Philadelphia Convention support the view that the great majority of the delegates did not favor the inclusion of the entire legislature in the treaty-making procedure.)

The Federal Convention spent most of its time working on the

---

[26] Madison, Notes, pp. 520-21, 597.

legislative function and its corresponding powers; which most delegates believed to be the most important as well as the dominant branch of Republican government. The Convention and public opinion were more divided over the executive and judicial branches and the powers to be assigned to those two branches of government. Consequently, the Founding Fathers wisely left to the First Congress (1789-91) the task of filling in the executive and judicial structures, duties, and limitations.

(This more concerned the judiciary than the executive.) The Convention never resolved the extent of executive power; Article II, Section 3, left room for both legislative and executive interpretation of the meaning of the "Presidency."

The "First Congress" spent most of its first session in organizing those two branches of government about which the Convention had made the fewest decisions. John Adams firmly opposed the aggrandizement of executive powers since he thought future Presidents might be liable to bribery and other misuses of office. Pierce Butler of South Carolina and Charles Carroll of Maryland, on the other hand, desired a strong President.

As noted above, the Convention spent relatively very little time on the question of the Judiciary; although James Madison believed that "An effective Judiciary establishment, commensurate to the legislative authority, was essential. A Government without a proper Executive & Judiciary would be the mere trunk of a body without arms or legs to act or move." There was also the question of jealousy between the supporters of state courts and the supporters of inferior federal courts. The Convention had been seriously divided on this subject. No one in the Convention opposed the creation of a "Supreme Court" which they all seemed to assume would rule on the constitutionality of state and national laws. Dispute did arise, however, over the question of inferior federal courts. John Rutledge, Roger Sherman, Nathaniel Gorham, Pierce Butler, Luther Martin, and George Mason opposed any inferior federal courts as an infringement on the states. Sherman believed that the state courts should serve as inferior federal courts. To nationalists like Madison, Wilson, and Morris, Sherman's position was an anathema. Edmund Randolph declared that the state courts could not be trusted to enforce the national authority. Although there was controversy on the subject, the Convention did approve, by a vote of eight to two, that the "National Congress" would have the power to create inferior federal courts at its discretion.

Article III of the Federal Constitution has been called one of the major compromises of the Convention; a compromise by postponement. As the creation of inferior federal courts was left to the "First Congress," so too was the jurisdictional disposition of judicial powers described in Article III Section 2 of the Federal Constitution. During the ratification of the Federal Constitution, the judiciary question created more controversy than it had during the Convention. Most common of the demands was that state courts should act as inferior courts and the "Admiralty courts" should be the only federal courts besides the "Supreme Court." Alexander Hamilton, whose proposals on the judiciary had been unacceptable to the Convention, wrote all the essays which dealt with the judiciary in The Federalist Papers (See particularly "Essay No. 78.") In those essays, Hamilton wrote that the "Federal Judiciary" would serve as a bulwark against state laws, which threatened private property as well as a defense against national authority."[27]

[27] Farrand, Debates , 1:124-27; John Adams, The Writings of John Adams , ed. Harry A. Cushing, 4 vols. (New York: G.P. Putnam's Sons, 1904-08), 1: 335-37.

V. CONCLUDING COMMENT

On September 17, 1787, Dr. Benjamin Franklin wrote a speech, which was read before the Convention by James Wilson, in which Franklin noted that he had various misgivings about the proposed Federal Constitution, but would sign it and support it since he thought that a "general government" was a necessity for the American people. He also remarked of his astonishment that "so near perfect Constitution" had been formulated and urged the other delegates to support it also. However, three delegates (Randolph, Mason, and Gerry) found reason not to sign the concluded document. Randolph noting that he felt it necessary "to be free to act for the public good." Nevertheless, the vast majority of the delegates, recognizing that the fate of the infant Republic depended upon the fruits of their efforts in Philadelphia, followed dr. Franklin's magnanimous initiative and did compromise many personal misgivings about the agreed-upon Constitution for the sake of the new Republic. The spirit of that compromise is nowhere more explicit than in the "Letter of Transmittal" of the new Constitution to the Congress. It reads as follows:

> . . . .The friends of our country have long seen and desired that the power of making war, peace, and treaties, that of levying money and regulating commerce, and the correspondent executive and judicial authorities should be

> fully and effectually vested in the general government of the Union: But the impropriety of delegating such extensive trust to one body of men is evident—Hence results the necessity of a different organization.
>
> In all our deliberations on this subject we kept steadily in our views, that which appears to us the greatest interest of every true American, the consolidation of our Union, in which is embodied our prosperity, felicity, safety, perhaps even our national existence. This important consideration, seriously and deeply impressed on our minds, led each state in the Convention to be less rigid on points of inferior magnitude, than might be expected and thus the Constitution, which we now present, is the result of a spirit of amity, and that of mutual deference and concession which the peculiarity of our political situation rendered indispensible . . . .[28]

Although the founding Fathers did not foresee the present day, rampant diffusion of bureaucratic functions among the three national branches, the "Doctrine of the Separation of Powers" and the correlative "Principle of Checks And Balances" still represent the essence of the American political experiment; as initially conceived in the Federal Convention in Philadelphia and as evolved in the present day transformation.

(Note: George Washington, by the unanimous consent of the assembled delegates, was chosen as the "Presiding Officer" of the "Constitutional Convention." By default, James Madison's copious "notes" became the official record of the Convention's proceedings.

Both John Adams and Thomas Jefferson did not go to Philadelphia;

---

[28] Tansill, Illustrative Documents , pp. 739-45, 1003-04.

as they were in Europe representing the American Government's interests. Patrick Henry also did not attend the Philadelphia Convention.

Dr. Franklin, however, did attend the Convention. He represented Pennsylvania and was the oldest delegate there.)

Comment:

The Question of "Presidential Impeachment":

Toward the final days of the "Constitutional Convention of 1787," the issue of "Presidential Impeachment" was discussed. Leading the discussion were James Madison, George Mason, and Edmond Randolph. On September 8, the only crimes for "Impeachment," up to that time, centered on "attempts to subvert the Constitution, Treason, and Bribery." But, on that day, George Mason, of Virginia, propose the now infamous phrase of "Other Crimes And Misdemeanors." (Borrowed from "English Impeachment Proceedings.") As noted, these were the final days of deliberation at the "Convention" and, perhaps, the delegates were tired and wanted to go home. In any event, they voted, eight states to two, to adopt the "The Removal of the Executive by Impeachment." (Which also included the "Other Crimes And Misdemeanors Addition.")

"Inside the Founding Fathers' Debate Over What Constituted An Impeachable Offense." (Erick Trickey, Smithsonian.Com, Oct.2, 2017); "What the Founders Thought About Impeachment And the President." (Scott Bamboy, May 18, 2017, "Constitution Daily," National Constitution Center.)

CURRICULUM VITAE
THOMAS E. SAWYER, Ph.D., J.D.

Military Service: United States Air Force; four years (Korean War).

U.S. Government Service: Twenty-three years of service as an "Operations Officer," "Clandestine Service," Central Intelligence Agency (CIA). While on active duty, served two tours of duty in Tehran, Iran; two tours in Asia; and two tours in Western Europe/Deputy Chief of Station at one post. (As a pilot, while in Iran, frequently flew with pilots of the Iranian Air Force.) While assigned to CIA Headquarters, traveled extensively overseas conducting operational matters. Taught at the university level; also was an Associate Research Professor—CPIA/SIS, American University. Served on academic panels discussing aspects of the Soviet political system and was associated with two "Consulting Firms" (wrote "project proposals" for U.S. Government contracts). After receiving his law degree, practiced law for fifteen years. Also served as president of a local "Bar Association" and, subsequently, as president of a regional "Bar Association." Also established and managed a commercial orchard; as well as managing timber property.

Education: Study of the Russian Language, The U.S. Air Force Russian Language Program, Syracuse University; B.A., Slavic Languages & Literature, University of California at Berkeley; M.A., Ph.D. ("With

Distinction"), Political Science, Georgetown University; and J.D., Washington College of Law, American University.

Publications: The Jewish Minority in the Soviet Union (Westview Press, Boulder, Col.; Wm. Dawson & Sons, Inc., Great Britain, 1979) which not only received international distribution, but also was recognized as an important reference source on the Soviet Jewish Issue. Moreover, after its publication the author received requests from individual professors at leading U.S., Canadian, and British universities seeking permission to use the book's data and other information in the classroom. Years later, copies of the book were still being sold by Amazon and "Book Stores" worldwide. Wrote book reviews, e.g., Thomas E. Sawyer, Review of "The Jews in the Soviet Union Since 1917," by Nora Levin in the Russian Review, Ohio State University, January 1993, pp. 117-18. Wrote articles for "Radio Liberty." Awarded a research grant from the "National Endowment for the Humanities" for research on the Soviet political system.

Now retired, the author and his wife, Ellen, currently reside somewhere in the Southwestern region of the United States.

SELECTED BIBLIOGRAPHY

Adams, John, Works. 10 vols. Boston: Little, Brown & Co., 1865.

Adams, Samuel. The Writings of Samuel Adams . Edited by Harry A. Cushing. 4 vols. New York: G.P. Putnam's Sons, 1904-1908.

Burns, Edward McNall. James Madison, Philosopher of the Constitution. New Brunswick, N.J.: Rutgers University Press, 1938.

Carey, George W. "A Separation of Powers & the Madisonian Model: A Reply to Critics." Georgetown University, 1976. (Typewritten.)

Corwin, Edward S. American Constitutional History. Edited by Alpheus T. Mason and Gerald Garvey. Gloucester, Mass.: Peter Smith, 1970.

Coxe, Brinton. An Essay on Judicial Power and Unconstitutional Legislation: Being a Commentary on Parts of the Constitution of the United States. Philadelphia: Kay and Brother, 1893.

Elliot, Jonathan. The Debates in the Several State Conventions on the Adoption of the Federal Constitution. 3rd ed. 5 vols. Philadelphia: J.B. Lippincott Co., 1901.

Farrand, Max, ed. The Records of the Federal Convention of 1787. 3 vols. New Haven: Yale University Press, 1937.

Hamilton, Alexander. The Works of Alexander Hamilton. Edited by Henry Cabot Lodge. 12 vols. New York: G.P. Putnam's Sons, 1904.

Hamilton, Alexander; Madison, James, and Jay, John. The Federalist Papers. Foreword by Clinton L. Rossiter. New York: New American Library, 1961.

Harvey, Ray F. The Political Philosophy of Jean Jacques Burlamaqui and His Relation to American Constitutional Theory . Chapel Hill: North Carolina University Press, 1937.

Henry, Patrick. Life, Correspondence, and Speeches. Edited by William Wirt. 3 vols. New York: B. Franklin, 1969.

Hunt, Gaillard, and Scott, James Brown, eds. The Debates in the Federal Convention of 1787 Which Framed the Constitution of the United States of America. New York: Oxford University Press, 1920.

Jefferson, Thomas. Notes on the State of Virginia. Edited by William Peden. Chapel Hill: University of North Carolina Press, 1955.

The Papers of Thomas Jefferson. Edited by Julian P. Boyd. 5 vols. Princeton: Princeton University Press. 1950—.

The Writings of Thomas Jefferson. Edited by Paul L. Ford. 10 vols. New York: G.P. Putnam's Sons, 1904.

Jensen Merrill. The Articles of Confederation: An Interpretation of the Social-Constitutional History of the American Revolution, 1774-1781. Madison: University of Wisconsin Press, 1948.

Locke, John. Two Treatises of Government. Cambridge: Cambridge University Press, 1960.

Madison, James. Notes of Debates in the Federal Convention of 1787. Introduction by Adrienne Koch: Athens: Ohio State University Press, 1966.

Montesquieu, Baron de. The Spirit of the Laws. Translated by Thomas Nugent. New York: Hafner Press, 1949.

Nevins, Allan. The American States During and After the Revolution, 1775-1789. New York: Macmillan Co., 1924.

Rossiter, Clinton Lawrence. Alexander Hamilton and the Constitution. New York: Harcourt, Brace & World, 1964.

Tansill, Charles C. Documents Illustrative of the Formation of the Union of the American States. Washington, D.C.: Government Printing Office, 1927.

Thorpe, Francis L. The Federal and State Constitutions, Colonial Charters, and Other Organic Laws. 7 vols. Washington, D.C.: Government Printing Office, 1907.

Vile, M.J.C. Constitutionalism and the Separation of Powers. Oxford: Clarendon Press, 1967.

Washington, George. The Writings of George Washington. Edited by John C. Fitzpatrick. 39 vols. Washington, D.C.: Library of Congress, 1931-44.

CPSIA information can be obtained
at www.ICGtesting.com
Printed in the USA
BVHW030806070321
601819BV00028B/521/J

9 781732 737167